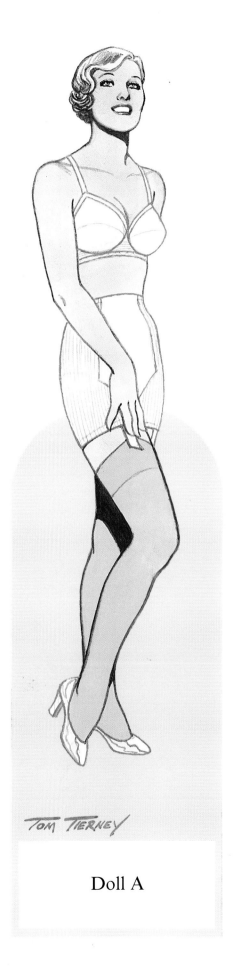

Doll A

Doll B

PLATE 1

Do not cut out space between arm and body.

CC

Claudette Colbert
It Happened One Night
1934

PLATE 2

Apply glue. Fold
over and fasten
to back of head,
creating pocket.

EL

EL

Tom Tierney

Elsa Lanchester
The Bride of Frankenstein
1935

Plate 3

Joan Crawford
The Bride Wore Red
1937

PLATE 4

GT

GT

Gene Tierney
The Razor's Edge
1946

PLATE 5

AH

Do not cut out space between arm and body.

AH

Tom Tierney

Audrey Hepburn
Funny Face
1957

PLATE 6

KR

Tom Tierney

Katharine Ross
The Graduate
1967

PLATE 7

TS

Talia Shire
The Godfather
1972

PLATE 8

RW

Tom Tierney

Robin Wright
The Princess Bride
1987

PLATE 9

Do not cut out
spaces between
arms and body.

SH

Shari Headley
Coming to America
1988

PLATE 10

MR

MR

Tom Tierney

Meg Ryan
Prelude to a Kiss
1992

PLATE 11

Toni Collette
Muriel's Wedding
1994

PLATE 12

JR

JR

Tom Tierney

Julia Roberts
Runaway Bride
1999

PLATE 13

Do not cut out
spaces between
arms and body.

Tom Tierney

Nia Vardalos
My Big Fat Greek Wedding
2002

PLATE 14

KK

KK

Keira Knightley
Love Actually
2003

PLATE 15